Unit 1

Friends
and Family

Contents

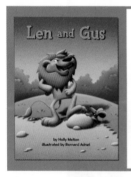

Pat and Tim

by Liane B. Onish
illustrated by Richard Torrey

Pat and Tim are pals. Both Pat and Tim like caps. Pat and Tim put on caps. Both caps fit. In a bit, Pat and Tim will play.

Pat and Tim like t-ball. Pat and Tim play for the Cats. There are blue caps for the Cats. Pat and Tim win!

Where are Pat and Tim? Tim has a cap. Pat has a yellow cap. Why can caps help?

4

It is a big day for Pat and Tim.
It is sad for the pals. Pat and Tim
go in even if they are sad.

Pat has Miss P. in 2-P. Tim has
Miss B. in 2-B. Pat will miss Tim.
Tim will miss Pat!

Len and Gus

by Holly Melton
illustrated by Bernard Adnet

The sun was hot. Gus could see lots of green on his jog.

Gus ran. Gus had fun. But Gus did not see Len!

"I got you!" said Len. "I was up on a big log."

"Let go! I beg you!" said Gus.

"If you let go, I can help you."

"How funny!" said Len. "You are not as big as a dog. How can one mouse help? But I will let go. Run, Gus, run!"

Gus ran.

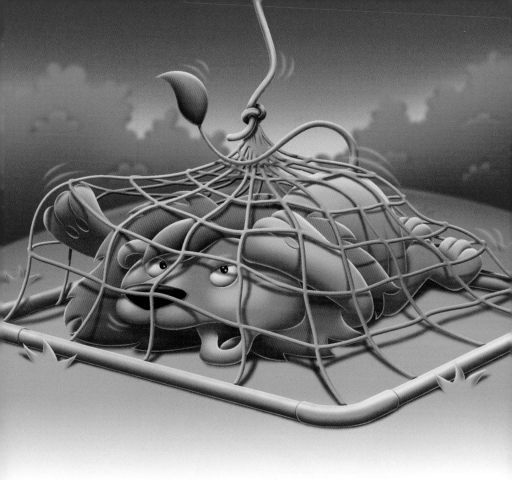

One day a big net fell on Len.
Len could not get up.

"HELP! Len said. "Men set a net.
I am like a bug in a web!"

Gus was on a jog. "It sounds like Len!" Gus said. "I can help him. It is a job for a mouse!"

Gus ran to find Len.

"I can help," said Gus. "I can cut the net."

"Get set and cut the net, or the men will get me!" said Len.

Gus got set. Gus bit the net. Gus bit and bit. The net was off! Len got up.

"You see," said Gus. A *little* mouse can help a *big* lion."

Spot

and
Fran

by Leslie A. Rotsky
illustrated by Roger Radtke

"Want to play?" asks Fran. Spot likes to play! Spot runs and gets twigs. He flips in the green grass.

"Stop! Stop!" yells Fran. But Spot can not stop.

Plop! Spot drops in the mud.
Spot has funny spots. Spot smells.
What can Fran do?

Fran has a plan. She grabs
a small tub and fills it up.

17

Spot hops in. He gets wet.
Fran rubs lots of suds on his spots.
But Spot can not sit still. He wants
to play.

Spot sees a boy and girl by the steps. Spot runs and trips on a pot. Plop! The pot spills on top of Spot.

"Where were you?" asks Fran. "What did you do?"

Fran grins at Spot. "You are a mess, but I am glad you are here."

"Want to play?" asks Fran.

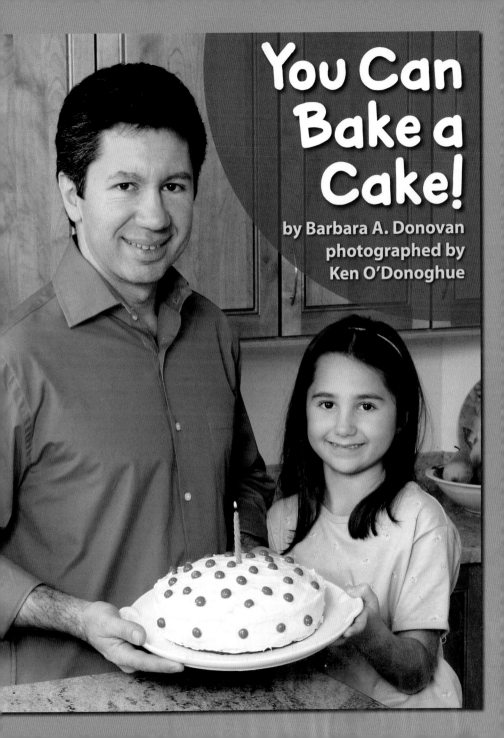

You Can Bake a Cake!

by Barbara A. Donovan
photographed by
Ken O'Donoghue

This year you and Dad can bake
a birthday cake for Mom. A cake is
fun to make. Dad has a cake mix.
Dad is glad he can help.

Ask Dad to set the oven. Grab
your cake pans. The cake mix
will go into the pans. Set up the
cake pans.

Get the cake box. Steps show how to make a cake. Mix the cake mix, water, and oil, too. Add an egg. Add another egg.

Dad can mix it up. Fill up the cake pans. Set the cake pans in a hot oven. You and Dad can sit and wait.

Let the cake bake. Move it to
a big plate. Frost the cake and dab
on red dots. Now you are done.
Mom is glad. Mom is going to take
this cake!

Mike's Big Bike

by Elena Matos
illustrated by Joe Cepeda

Mike rides his small bike.
As it moves, his legs hit the
handlebars. Mike likes his bike, but
he understands it is not the right
size. What will Mike do?

Mike tells Mom he has to get a big bike. Mom will help Mike pay for it. Mike will save up, too.

Mike gets to work. He rakes twigs. He cuts grass.

Mike has a sale. He wipes the grill. He fixes a man's kite. He works at other jobs. Mike saves up.

Now Mike can get a fine new
bike. Mike goes to Mr. Hide's sale.
Mike sits on a green bike. He rides
all of the bikes. Mike finds a bike
he likes. It is the right size and the
right price. Mike gets a red bike.
It is a big bike!

Mike rides his red bike. Tim asks to ride it. Mike says, "You ride the big bike. I will ride the small bike. I can ride my big bike any time!" Mike and Tim smile.

Unit 1: Friends and Family

to use with *Little Flap Learns to Fly*   **WORD COUNT: 121**

DECODABLE WORDS
Target Phonics Elements
short *a*
and, cap, caps, Cats, has, Pat, pals, sad
short *i*
bit, fit, in, is, it, miss, Tim, will, win

HIGH-FREQUENCY WORDS
ball, blue, both, even, for, help, put, there, why, yellow
Review: a, are, do, like, play, to, they

STORY WORDS
day

33

to use with *Maria Celebrates Brazil*   **WORD COUNT: 190**

DECODABLE WORDS

Target Phonics Elements

   short *e*

      beg, fell, get, Len, let, men, net, set, web

   short *o*

      dog, got, hot, job, jog, log, lots, not, off, on

   short *u*

      but, cut, fun, Gus, run, sun, up

HIGH-FREQUENCY WORDS

   could, find, funny, green, how, little, one, or, see, sounds

   Review: and, are even, for, go, help, like, me, of, said, the, this, to, was, you

STORY WORDS

   day, lion, mouse

to use with *Finding Cal*   **WORD COUNT: 137**

DECODABLE WORDS
Target Phonics Elements
   r-blends
      drops, Fran, frog, grabs,
      grass, green, grins
   s-blends
      small, smells, spot, spots, steps,
      spills, still
   t-blends
      trips, twigs
   l-blends
      play, flips, plop, glad

HIGH-FREQUENCY WORDS
   boy, by, girl, he, here, she, small, want, were, what
   Review: and, are, do, funny, green, like, of, sees, the, to, where, you

STORY WORDS
   asks

to use with *Taking Care of Pepper* **WORD COUNT: 140**

DECODABLE WORDS
Target Phonics Elements
short *a*
add, an, ask, can, Dad, dab, grab, pans
long *a: a_e*
bake, cake, cakes, make, plate, same, take

HIGH-FREQUENCY WORDS
another, done, into, move, now, show, too, water, year, your
Review: and, are, do, find, for, go, help, like, on, put, some, this, to, what, you

STORY WORDS
birthday, oil, oven, wait

to use with *Families Work!*   **WORD COUNT: 176**

DECODABLE WORDS

Target Phonics Elements

short *i*

big, fixes, grill, his, hit, is, it, twigs, this, Tim, will

long *i*

bike, bikes, fine, Hide's, kite, likes, Mike, ride, rides, size, smile, time, wipes

HIGH-FREQUENCY WORDS

all, any, goes, new, number, other, right, says, understands, work

Review: and, do, finds, for, has, he, help, moves, my, now, of, small, the, to, too, what, you

STORY WORDS

handlebars, pay, price

HIGH-FREQUENCY WORDS TAUGHT TO DATE

Grade K	Grade I					Grade 2
a	about	change	house	orange	three	and
and	across	climbed	how	other	through	are
are	after	come	instead	our	today	do
can	again	could	into	out	together	go
do	against	does	it	over	too	has
for	air	done	jump	people	two	like
go	all	down	knew	place	under	me
has	along	early	know	poor	until	my
have	also	eat	laugh	pretty	up	of
he	always	eight	learn	pull	upon	on
here	another	enough	live	put	use	play
I	any	every	love	ride	very	said
is	around	eyes	make	run	walked	some
like	away	fall	many	saw	want	the
little	ball	father	minutes	says	warm	they
look	be	find	more	school	water	this
me	because	four	mother	searching	way	to
my	been	friends	move	should	were	was
play	before	from	never	shout	who	where
said	begin	full	new	show	why	you
see	below	funny	no	so	work	
she	better	girl	not	some	would	
the	blue	give	nothing	soon	write	
this	boy	goes	now	sound	yellow	
to	brought	gone	of	straight	your	
was	build	good	old	sure		
we	buy	great	once	their		
what	by	grew	one	then		
where	call	head	only	there		
with	carry	help	open	they		
you	certain	her	or	thought		

38

DECODING SKILLS TAUGHT TO DATE

CVC letter patterns; short *a*; consonants *b, c, ck, f, g, h, k, l, m, n, p, r, s, t, v*; inflectional ending *-s* (plurals, verbs); short *i*; consonants *d, j, qu, w, x, y, z*; double final consonants; *l* blends; possessives with *'s*; end blends; short *o*; inflectional ending *-ed*; short *e*; contractions with *n't*; *s* blends; *r* blends; inflectional ending *-ing*; short *u*; contractions with *'s*; digraphs *sh, th, ng*; compound words; long *a (a_e)*, inflectional ending *-ed* (drop final *e*); long *i (i_e)*; soft *c, g, -dge*; digraphs *ch, -tch, wh-, ph*; inflectional ending *-es* (no change to base word); long *e (e_e)*, long *o (o_e)*, long *u (u_e)*; silent letters *gn, kn, wr*; 3-letter blends *scr-, spl-, spr-, str-*; inflectional endings *-ed, -ing* (double final consonant); long *a (ai, ay)*; inflectional endings *-er, -est*; long *e (e, ea, ee, ie)*; *e* at the end of long *e* words; long *o (o, oa, oe, ow)*; 2-syllable words; long *i (i, ie, igh, y)*; 2-syllable inflectional endings (changing *y* to *ie*); long *e (ey, y)*; inflectional ending *-ed* (verbs; change *y* to *i*); *r*-controlled vowel /ûr/*er, ir, ur*; inflectional endings *-er, -est* (drop final *e*); *r*-controlled vowel /är/ *ar*; abbreviations Mr., Mrs., Dr.; *r*-controlled vowel /ôr/*or, oar, ore*; *ea* as short *e*; diphthong /ou/ *ou, ow*; final *e* (mouse, house); diphthong /oi/*oi, oy*; prefixes *re-, un-*; variant vowels /ù /*oo*, /ü/*oo, ew, ue, u_e, ou*; possessives; variant vowel /ô/*a, au, aw, augh*; singular and plural possessive pronouns; 2-syllable words; *r*-controlled vowel /âr/*air, are, ear*; contractions; open syllables; closed syllables; final stable syllables; vowel digraph syllables; *r*-controlled vowel syllables; vowel diphthong syllables; short *a, e, i, o, u*; consonant blends *dr, sl, sk, sp, st*; consonant digraphs *ch, -tch, sh, th, wh, ph*; long *a (a_e)*, *i (i_e)*, *o (o_e)*, *u (u_e)*; soft *c* and *g*

39